LO͞O͞KING
AT
EACH OTHER

or

Orpheus Re-Cycled: The Perils of Reciprocal Oculation

First published (as a pocket-paperback): 2023
This illustrated edition: 2024

ISBN: 978-1-73857-420-9

To my wife Lois
with love and gratitude

———————————————

Robin and I would also like to dedicate this edition to our brother Nick,
immortalised on page 4 as the face of Orpheus
confronted with 'that foreign finger thing'.

Battle Hymn of the Breakaway

Through and off, through and off, through and off.
Though thighs do burn miss not a turn.
Through and off, through and off, through and off.
Though crosswinds blow, stick with the flow.
Through and off, through and off, through and off.
Though tempers fray, no tempos may.
Through and off, through and off, through and off.
Enjoy the view.. but no can do.
Through and off, through and off, through and off.
In time of trial, just think time trial.
Through and off, through and off, through and off.
Phew! Caught at last, caught and passed,
Had enough through and off. Through! (And off.)

Robin Reynolds
2023

LOOKING AT EACH OTHER

Départ réel

The break's been out all day,
Hopes to make it all the way.
Though the chase behind is keen,
The peloton full of spleen
And hungry to make the catch,
These six out front still could snatch
The stage. But it will be tight –
All are working, as is right
If they want to split the spoil
(Just reward for honest toil)…
Now what? Oh no! Oh brother!
They're looking at each other!
All is lost, the bunch sweeps by,
For a sprinters' do-or-die.

Another boot, the other foot.
This time things are looking moot
For the breakaway: barely
Two minutes and, unfairly,
Thirty K. Fishes in play,

But that's bike racing, they say:
Slog on, all hope abandon.
Meanwhile in the peloton,
Time for a snack and a nap…
Attack! Keen to bridge the gap,
Two rogues snap the elastic.
This brings a new dynamic:
Their teams sit up (why bother?),
The rest *look at each other!*
Now the break with extra legs
Steals all the bacon-and-eggs.

Mutual admiration:
Is it mere superstition?
Or does it truly snooker
Hopes for the short-term future?
Why should exchanges of glance
With rivals (or friends perchance)
Bring ill fortune by and by?

Now, though no cycling pro I,
(Never raced a Grenadier
Nor dodged a Quick-Step rapier) [1]
I have noticed in cov'rage
Is said much more than av'rage:
They're looking at each other.
Helped by a late grandmother, [2]
I found out where it started:
This tale of lovers parted,
A myth of Hellenic yore.
Attend; you've a treat in store...

Départ fictif

To the Tour de Tartarus
Rides our hero Orpheus.
Black is the tint – says hearsay –
Of the General jersey, [3]
And as for KOM, it's
Known as the Boss of the Pits. [4]

A stage is what O's after,
One for music and laughter...
Well, music at any rate.

Eurydice was his mate
Until her death them did part.
Snakebite it was stopped her heart,
But – before you pass judgement –
She did tread on that serpent.
Orpheus wants her back home,
So braves this dark catacomb
Hoping Hades he'll persuade
To return his darling maid
(Yeah right! But to save the rhyme,
We'll let it go, just this time).

The old Underworld god likes
Lyres and puns as well as bikes;
Orpheus sings some songs he's writ,
Hades is suitably smit
By the greatest lyre, self-styled,
Of all time (except unwhiled:
What is the future if not
Time – its still ravelled reef knot?)
And gives his stern permission
With one little condition.
'Time-trial out, monsieur,' says he.

'On your wheel Eurydice
Shall ride. Focus, take no risk.
Head down, chin up, cadence brisk,
No arm flick to share the breeze,
No pre-line peek to check she's
There – that's your real deal-breaker!
Eyes front, or no meal-maker!'
*(My apologies, ladies,
For the Jurassic Hades.)*

'Talking of brakes – yours, tsk tsk!
Not rim but newfangled disc?
It'll never catch on, you'll find!
Ha ha! Geddit? Never mind!
Ma foi! Chacun son [*sic*] roue! [5]
Hades sports a Gallic hue
For his Tour *de* Tartarus.
His grammar may torture us,
And some call it affected.
Tant pis! is his elected
Retort. Eager to please, though,
Orpheus replies 'Plutôt!'
'Pluto! That's gonna cost yer!

Name that Roman imposter
Would you, in *my* Underworld? [6]
Allez! Get out! – Go *un*girled,'
Cries Hades, anger uncorked.

Poetically pitchforked
And altogether unmanned
By such a blow to his planned
Return of bliss late enjoyed,
O's fragile spirits, unbuoyed,
Collapse right there on the ramp.
Hades, anxious to decamp,
(And also dimly aware
He misunderstood back there)
Relents, which amps his stature.
Then, as TT dispatcher,
He does that foreign finger
Thing, counting-down the singer –
A low trick, to say the least!
But at last they're off like greased
Lightning. Not one of your neg
ative splitters while a leg

◀ *Not cricket: that foreign finger thing.*

ROBIN REYNOLDS
2023

Alive and pedals he has,
Orpheus goes out full gas. [7]

⊙⊙

This dark time-trial *parcours*
(A French word, meaning parcours)
Includes sections of cobbles,
Ice, sand and other troubles
Along the nine infernal
Hairpins of Dante's journal.
The twists and turns are narrow,
And choked with fans who harrow,
Harass and harry all who
Hardly manage the haul through
Lit'ral pandemonium.

Despite disharmonium
With Hades on the question
Of doctrine and religion,
The Devil always shows up.
Whatever the race throws up,
You'll see him, brandishing his
Great trident and whishing his

Wicked tail, in case the cruel
Capricious Lord of Misrule*
(*See 'Julian Calendar'),
Once more nick his 'Befriender',
As he, in ironic quotes,
Calls the prongs on which he dotes. [8]

Round the bend a merry troupe
Of soothsayers wait and whoop.
One genial chap makes hay
With fierce Béla's sobriquet [9]
(Whose clay's long safely mortal)
And with a cheery chortle
Games names from the peloton –
'Making waves is Fred Frison',
'And that's Tadej's news today',
'Pacher looks costly, I'd say',
*'Here comes Hoover, cleaning up
The points'* – never shutting up!

Though one wily vet drily
Jokes (eyes a-twinkle slyly)
That she's on track to dowse all
Sparks of verbal carousal,

It seems none can suppress him.
He himself declares, bless him,
She will never curb his glee,
For he'll be no one's curbee.

Now, the Music of the Spheres
Back in the background one hears.
Listen... in honeyed verses,
Polly van Glot rehearses
Names as native-intended:
Vowels mystic'ly blended
With consonants, fricatives
And nasal prohibitives.

Riders our Poll announces,
Syllables true pronounces.
'Eduardo Sepúlveda,
Torstein Traeen, Évita
Muzic, Cecilie Uttrup
Ludwig, Pierre-Pascal Keup,
Marta Cavalli, Stine
Borgli, Sylvain Moniquet,
Chawchiangkwang, Jake Stewart,
Floortje Mackaij, Wout Van Aert'

Shimmer in the inner ear
And, ennobled, fade to air.

Next to be found of this theme:
A double-act, the dream team –
Reverie and Revelrie.
Reverie is the dreamy
One: he tells, sans elisions,
His intricate bright visions
Of flag-to-line stage races.

Revelrie the Sage traces
Through his pardner's mystery
The fault lines of History
And Destiny, explaining
(*Snark fans, please, no complaining*) [10]
The state of the lore in round,
Soft undercurrents of sound.

(A Giromancer of old, [11]
Spinning yarns as Worlds unfold,
This Legend of the Saddle
Despises fiddle-faddle.
And despite his moniker

Hinting at cheer and liquor,
In truth no wild raver he:
His name, ending in i, e,
Accounts him Revelator.
Hence, Y, thou partygator!) [12]

A little apart, stage right,
A beautiful anchorite
Sits silent, grave, demure,
All aloof yet all allure.
All adore her, all agog
For her daily analogue.

As she weaves in thought her next
Predictive textile, complex
Silks and stuffs self-assemble
Into her day's ensemble,
Cottons and stretchy things too,
Of lacy linens no few.

Her raiment is her glory,
Each outfit tells a story
From her supple subtle mind:
In thread and colour defined –
Vivid as chromatophores

On a dawn-dancing seahorse – [13]
Fate and fortune for the stage,
Who will cheer and who will rage.

Striped green socks? A gentle hint
To expect a wild bunch sprint;
Yellow boots? a GC lead;
Polka tank-top?... but no need
To go on and on! You get
The idea (or will do yet).

Right, that's the colour bit done.
Now for some frantic action:
Our often under-rated
Poet, as above-stated,
Flies away like a missile
And it takes his miss a while
To close the gap. Luckily –
Though she hides it craftily
(*The frail ego of the male,
Aka moral blackmail*) –
She is the superior
Bike handler (the eerier
Too, given that she is dead).

◄ *A beautiful anchorite, all allure.*

Though heedless he drives ahead,
She's on his wheel soon enough,
And at no great cost in puff.

The obsidian pavé
Sees 'em just about half way,
Rattled and bounced, but as yet
Far from trounced, for these glass-set
Cobbles, although malicious,
Have to resign their vicious
Japes today to the gravel
That the lovers must travel.

Those chippings feel they are due
A spiteful puncture or two –
'The well-laid have all the fun,'
They complain, 'but there's a ton
We Loosers have to offer
In tumbling racers off their
Bikes in new and novel ways,
Mechanical ploys and plays;
A well-placed stone, a rear tyre...
Oops! cracked visor back there, squire?'

Into some shingle Orph ploughs,
Spitting out a few choice vows
(Down there they curse in reverse;
Why? Hades quips it's *obverse*!).
He skids, crashes and starts to slide,
Gouging and shredding his hide
As, helpless, he spins to find
Himself looking straight behind,
Where Eurydice should be –
But is not, mercifully!
He sees, parked neatly, her bike;
Of course! a quick nature hike.
Relieved, he slowly remounts
And pedals ahead. He counts
On her to catch him again,
Not hard on tricky terrain.

In fact, the biggest danger
To the deal that could change her
Vital status, lurks within
The coils of those tight hairpin
Bends. Doing a one-eighty
Multiplies the odds greatly

That the forbad will be seen
Once you face back where you've been.
This puzzling perplexity
Resolves with convexity:
Eurydice corners wide
As he turns, on his blind side,
Scarily close but outside
His arc, remaining unspied.

That is hard to do, of course,
Drains ev'ry ounce of resource.
But luckily as they rise
The crowd increases in size:
Folk and flags drape the sidelines,
Masking those fickle sight-lines,
And stem with their density
Her labour intensity.

Orpheus oblivious
Rides on – punctilious
But close to total collapse.
As the milk in his legs saps
His will, he prays for his want.
'Your prayer is important

To us,' he hears. 'But all our
Angels are busy this hour.'

Then, when he's about to faint,
Thomas of Gendt (patron saint
Of the Breakaway, Stoic
Bold and Beard Beatific)
Shows up, as ever he's wont,
For a long pull at the front.

Drafting behind the holy
Hero, Orph repents wholly
His spineless moral failure
Of a few minutes earlier –
Perhaps because his lactic
Tics ease, as if by magic…

So when their guide, with a nod,
Leaves them to the final plod,
Orpheus, for redemption,
Tackles the steep ascension
With promiscuous vigour.
But he omits to figure

Whether Eurydice's legs
Might not be on their last dregs
Of spirit and stamina:
The work she can cram in a
Few hours is not infinite
And those bends found her limit.
So when he jumps like the Shark [14]
She's a bit slow off the mark.
(It's just a testosterone
Burst – but, yes, a scary one
For her, all taken aback
By Orphy's sudden attack.)

Unable to close it down,
She names him a naughty noun
And, revived by her anger
At his tactical clanger,
She pictures him skinned alive,
Then gathers her wind to strive,
If not to catch, then to match
At least his tactless dispatch:
Enough to keep him in view
And recoup a sec or two.

She has the heart of the crowd,
But their support is too loud,
Behind the barriers now,
Which they bang, making a row
That drowns out her anguished shout:
'Oi! Orpheus, hang about!'

All the gods from Olympus –
A *posse comitatus* – [15]
Are in town for a summit
To defy or to submit
To a demand, from chis'ling
Lawyers for the bullying
Rulers of the ancient Games,
That Zeus's pantheon change
The name of his mountain home.
They claim it infringes some
Trade mark, brand or copyright
Hold on 'Olymp' terms – by might
Enforced, not by right or sense!
(Not that I have aught against
Copyright, you understand:

Mainly it's the concept 'brand',
Misapplied, that burns me up.)

I digress: all that wind up,
And just to say that a few
Of those gods, also a crew
Of their Latin counterparts
And other snooty braggarts,
Have come to the finish line
Expressly to undermine,
Never to praise or support
(Crashes are *such* jolly sport!).

Eurydice wants to cry
When she hears through the noise, 'I
Want to ride my bicycle,
I want to ride my bike!'... 'Well!'
She fumes, 'that's a famous voice,
But not a patch on my boy's...
Why of course! It's Mercury –
Same old jealous mockery [16]
From a frustrated junior
Deity who's no tunier
Than a cat. Wings on his hat

And boots! Cost him a ducat
Or two, or whatever coins
Rome has. He should dress his loins
Instead! And those footflaps must
Tangle in his chain' – unjust
Disgust with every huff!

(Mercury is better stuff
Than she gives him credit for:
Great pops vox, Sub-Editor
(A newspaper's Jedi core,
Before we forget it all)
On *Messaggero degli
Dei* – plus, speaking legly, [17]
Breeches might bust his headlines,
And circumvent his bylines.)

But grumbling keeps her going,
With Orpheus still flowing
Fast towards a finish arch
That's fit for a triumph march:
Marble, natch, nowt inflated
(Except its overstated
Sense of Hades' importance).

But at any rate, Orphy
Is almost home, his Trophy
Reclaimed and back in his bed
(That's how things are in his head).
He buttons his shirt (no zips
Back then) and, arms on high, slips
Across the line, supposing
His loved one close or closing.

At last, he feels free to smile
Into her eyes, to beguile
Her re-beating heart, to dare
To dream of a future where
They live again as man and
Wife, as woman and husband.
(Technically, of course, they
Are now single: wedding day
Vows expire on expiry –
'Till death' and all that miry
Small print – and Eurydice
Had certainly died. But we
Pass on: it's moot anyway,
As these couplets soon portray.)

So Orpheus glances right:
No Eurydice. A slight
Frown, and he looks to his left:
Not there; he starts to fear theft
(Of bike) or kidnap (of wife)
By some afterlife lowlife.
In a panic he swings round,
Thinking to pursue the hound.
Aghast, he sees her a few
Yards *short* of the line; she too
Is aghast – their very last
Shared emotion. The steadfast
Hope in her eyes is displaced
By despair, meeting his, laced
With guilty dews; she barely
Hears the frantic crowd tearly
Crying 'No no no! Oh lover!
They're looking at each other!'

Her chain breaks, both tyres explode,
The frame twists, she hits the road,
Horror and love, terror and rage
Mingling on her final page.

Her panting bosom quickens
As within, her heart sickens.
Yet in darkling she finds grace,
Enough to forgive the face
Of the sentimental dope
Who brought her the joy of hope
Renewed. (Hope, ha! Fickle friend
Who betrayed them in the end.)

That same dope, barred by hands
Unseen from touching her, stands
Rigid as her life dissolves.
On her bike there revolves
One lonely pedal, awry,
Spinning slowly down... [18]

OO

Dying's hard and the second
Time is commonly reckoned
Worse than the first; after that
It quickly becomes old hat.
'The later, the better bet' –
So preach Death's dead-setter set.
Of this, Hades is aware –

Of course – lateness is his sphere!
But he's early on this scene,
Keen to act callous and mean.

From the Race Director's red
Chariot, its steeds undead,
With a camp flourish he vaults,
Toga in the wind, no shorts –
Picture Bacchus by Titian [19]
(Clear mythappropriation,
That painting: said debaucher
Was Dionysus for sure,
Rake of the canon Grecian,
Not derivative Roman.)

So, landing with a stagger,
The god regains his swagger
And, modestly insincere,
Gasps 'Oof! Getting old, I fear.'
Then gives the singer a slap
On the back, the kind a chap
Takes in good part if a sport.
Orpheus hates it a mort
(And not just 'cause his dorsal

One lonely pedal. ▶

Skin is about as sore's all
Get-out – bloodied, bruised and raw
After his brush with the law
Of gravity). An old crate
Hades finds for the twice-late
Eurydice, Orph-baiting
As he stuffs her in: 'Dating?
You're available, I hear!
Why not try those two up there?'
He cracks his whip and is borne
Off with the remains. Forlorn
Orph stands, till that parting leer
Goads his grudging gaze 'up there'...

👀

Of course, he stands not a chance
With this pair – looking askance
At his stare – as Hades knew
Very well. For these are two
Proud ladies: Hanna the Meek
(She who shall inherit eke [20]
The earth and all its rainbows), [21]
And one on whom *would* rain beaux,

Could they but catch her off-bike:
Fair Maid Marian, saintlike
Champion of the greenwood
Where she honed her skills real good,
Making fools of the sheriff's
Team, tying them all up in Notts,
Saving with her band of she-Riffs
Robin Hood's men in tight spots –
Not once but time and again.

Always up for a campaign,
She upsets the old order,
Will dispute any border,
Brave even the slur 'outlaw',
To share prizes with the poor,
To turn, with polite outrage,
Disvantage to advantage.

Now Marian states: 'A rule
Is a rule, and though you'll
Think that harsh, as a rule it
Should apply. Bite the bullet,
Bear the bitter bleak blemish
Brightly, as befits beamish

The death of hope. ▶

Bike-buddies blatantly blessed
By backbone.' Hanna, in jest:
'I thought you took a hands-off
Position on rules?' 'Lay off
The commissaires, I say!' laughs [22]
Her friend, who does nix by halfs.

Then sombrely: 'These events
Have stained our sweet innocence.
Henceforth this sport, I predict,
Will suffer for its looks. Tricked
Out of our polite "You first",
"No no, after you", we're cursed
To regard invitation
As tiltyard vacillation.

Oculation is Bad Luck [23]
Officially – trumping pluck
And hard work. From this day on,
I promise, in peloton
Or break, you'll not discover
Me looking at each other.'
'Never?' 'Well... hardly ever.'
Hanna concurs: 'And never –

Not even hurt or sickly –
Shall anybody catch me!' [24]

OO

But what of our heroine?
To a stats table, wherein
(As if dying weren't enough!)
We find this slight epitaph:
Eurydice – DNF.   [25]

The world and all its rainbows. ▶

Endnotes

1. Grenadier and Quickstep are shorthand references (at the time of writing) to two World Tour cycling teams.

2. Sorry, Grannies both, but I needed the rhyme.

3. Hearsay because nobody has ever seen it. It's dark down there, so black is pretty much invisible. We therefore *infer* black, because any other colour would show up at least a bit. It's an example of an apodictic statement: one we know to be true although it can't be tested.

4. KOM stands for King of the Mountains, a subsidiary competition to find the best climber of the race, who is rewarded with a polka-dot jersey. A requirement that a red nose be worn along with the dotty jersey never really caught on. Anyway, down in Tartarus climbing is seen as something for those who aspire to the heavens, whereas Tartarans prefer to honour the art of reckless descending.

5. That [*sic*] is part of the line and indispensable to the metre, not to mention to the rhyme and the joke. It is intended to be 'sounded', whether reading silently or out loud. I could have written [*sic*][*sic*] to make it clearer, I suppose, but was afraid of seeming pretentious.

6. Hades is being Disambiguous here. In his plutophobic eagerness to Dis his rival/alter-ego, he sometimes strays from the mythological truth, which is that Pluto was originally Hellenic (his very name – Πλούτωνας – is Greek after all) but at some uncertain point he switched to the Latin sponsor – no doubt for an exorbitant transfer fee.

7. A 'negative split' is the tactical containment of effort over the first half of a course to enable the rider to go 'full gas' into the finish.

8. Some fans of the Tour de France like to make themselves conspicuous in outlandish costumes – pandas and what have you. Since 1993, 'Didi the Devil' has bedevilled the race every year, bar one or two when he had to abandon through ill health, and has become a popular fixture with riders, commentators and fans – both roadside and sofaside. In 2018 (I think), in the Pyrenees, Julian Alaphilippe snatched Didi's trident as he passed and bore it aloft for a short distance. The incident was mentioned after-the-fact in commentary but was not caught on camera... or was it?

9. Most likely (I think, after checking Wikipedia) Béla IV (of V), 1206–1270, king in a turbulent time of Hungary and Croatia.

10. From *The Hunting of the Snark*, by Lewis Carroll:
    > And the Judge kept explaining the state of the law
    > In a soft under-current of sound.

11. A pun on 'gyromancer', a member of that order of mystics once called 'whirling dervishes', now better known as 'spin doctors'.

12. 'Hence why...' is a source of bitter controversy: whole pedant families have been put asunder by it. Puritanical purists denounce it as pleonasm or even tautology (and there's yet another rift-within-a-rift). I shan't detain you with the arguments, but personally I think it a healthy idiom, and in any case its use boasts a legal precedent. In October 2022, Judge Richard Marks KC, speaking in a soft undercurrent of sound, used it when jailing Jemma Mitchell for the murder of Mee Kuen Chong: 'This [a puncture] meant that you had rather less time,' he said, ' ... to find a place to secrete the body than you had envisaged. Hence why you were unable to find a more remote location than you did.' I rest m'case, m'lud.

13. My thanks to Katherine Rundell, whose essential (and delightful) book *The Golden Mole* gave me that glorious image of the amorous seahorse who starts his day by flashing his chromatophores at his lady-love.

14. The recently-retired Italian rider Vincenzo Nibali was known as 'the Shark' and had a propensity for the sudden, dramatic surge off the front.

15. 'Posse comitatus' is a Latin expression signifying essentially an empowered committee, a committee that *can*, rather than one that merely proposes (*cant*, as it were). Specifically, a 'force of the county', raised

by the Sheriff for a temporary purpose such as to subdue riot or chase bad guys. Thus, but for the caprice and fortune of linguistic evolution, Butch might have said to Sundance: 'Dang! There's that committee again, hard on our trail.'

[16] At the risk of being cancelled at the stake for heresy, I think *Bicycle Race* by Queen *does* poke fun at bike racing, at least in part. It paints a picture of an anti-social individual with no interest in cool stuff like *Jaws* and *Star Wars*, and with a similar disregard for public convenience when roads are closed so that the cyclist can 'ride it where I like'. Just saying.

[17] *'Messenger of the Gods'*. But you knew that already.

[18] A reference to the line 'If the world should stop revolving, spinning slowly down to die', from *If* by David Gates and Bread, 1971 (though I am more familiar with Cleo Laine's 1997 version).

[19] *Bacchus and Ariadne*, by the Venetian artist Titian, a major figure of the Renaissance. It is the one where the god and his retinue take the jilted Ariadne by surprise as she gazes forlornly after the ships disappearing over the horizon with her faithless partner Theseus. Wikipedia claims that Bacchus/Dionysus is leaping from his chariot to protect her from his wild cheetahs, but that is clearly a feeble pretext. I mean, look at those pussy cats: they're showing more interest in the view than in the woman.

[20] Eke, a good old word meaning 'both' / 'also', depending on context. Marked archaic in the 2011 Concise Oxford, at least it's still in there. Not to be confused with the verb 'to eke', meaning to stretch out, as in 'We must eke out our footnotes to get some actual poetry into Amazon's Look Inside feature.'

[21] The Dutch rider Annemiek van Vleuten made a habit of winning almost every race she entered, including four world championships (two road-race, two time-trial – *contre la montre*, as Hades would say) collecting for each a 'rainbow' jersey, so-called for the multicoloured band around the middle. The five (not

seven) colours are in the wrong order for a true rainbow, but only a benighted pedant would worry about that.

[22] Marianne Vos, another dominant Dutch figure in the women's peloton and the inspiration for my English Maid Marian, was disqualified after winning the one-day Postnord Vårgårda road race in Sweden in August 2022. In a momentary lapse of concentration she had ridden briefly in the 'puppy paws' position – wrists resting on the handlebars, weary hands flopping in front – which is a self-indulgence forbidden by the UCI. It can have been no more than a few seconds before she recovered her presence of mind and resumed the officially approved position of hands on the controls, but the sin was caught on camera. Ever-gracious, she accepted her penalty without demur and acknowledged [I paraphrase] that she had officially crossed the line, forfeiting the right to cross the line officially.

[23] 'Oculation' is not a word you'll find in the dictionary (at least, not in any of mine), an oversight that I am prepared to overlook. It's logical enough: we have 'ocular' (pertaining to vision) and the adjective 'oculate' (adorned with eye-like spots). Not to be confused with 'osculation' – reciprocal osculation is a wholly beneficial occupation with (in and of itself) no harmful effects (black eyes from jealous rivals don't count).

[24] Ms van Vleuten won the road-race rainbow at the 2022 world championships in Australia two days *after* breaking an arm in a freak accident coming off the starting ramp for the team time-trial. Earlier that year she had taken the yellow jersey in the inaugural Tour de France Femmes (avec Zwift, natch) despite losing a lot of early time (and much else besides) because of a crippling tummy bug.

[25] Did Not Finish.

Acknowledgements

Barbara Rundell, whose enthusiasm after reading an early draft encouraged me wonderfully. (I've since learned that at the time she was laid up with a painful foot injury, and *any* distraction would have been welcome!)

Sonia Charbonnier, who in addition to designing both this and the pocket-paperback edition of Looking At Each Other, has provided invaluable help and advice as I embark on the murky adventure of self-publishing.

The Greater Peloton, by which I mean not just those directly involved – riders, crew, organisers and so on – but also people like the media (yes they do, sometimes!), sponsors, fans (roadside and couchside), all of whom constitute the marvellous microcosm wherein I have staged my fond fancies, and without whose unwitting contributions I might have had to make stuff up. Some of my characters were inspired by a few of the (many) larger-than-life denizens of that region, but I must piously stress that any resemblance to real persons, living, dead or legendary, is coincidental and entirely (to a first approximation) unintended...

Printed in Great Britain
by Amazon

40716921R00021